The Higgs Boson and Other Phenomena

48 Poems

by

Michael Estabrook

for Patti

Acknowledgements

Some of these poems have appeared in the following journals, both online and in print:

Aberration Labyrinth, Angry Old Man, Challenger, Eclectica Magazine, Evening Street Review, Ibbetson Street Press, Jitter Press, Joey & the Black Boots the ReBOOT, Kalyna Review, Leaves of Ink, Literary Orphans, MadSwirl, Nerve Cowboy, Nine Muses Poetry, Pif Magazine, Poetry Quarterly, Red Booth Review, Rockhurst Review, Sheila-Na-Gig Online, Slipstream, Steam Ticket, Straight Forward Poetry, Taj Mahal Review, Terrene, The Bond Street Review, The Café Review, The Cape Rock, The Mystic Blue Review, The Saturday Diner, Thorny Locust, White Ash Magazine, Wilderness House Literary Review.

Contents

Another Quarrel 7

Wormholes 8

The Big Bang 10

Metaphysics 11

King Arthur Died in AD 538 12

Ruins 14

Michelangelo's David (1501-1504) 17

Gelato 20

Reality 21

Blaise Pascal (1623-1662) 22

Hell is empty and all the devils are here. 23

Existentialism 25

Swarm Bots 26

Higgs Boson 28

From Nothing 30

Moonlight 31

History of Midnight 32

Can't Find You 34

What If? 36

New Year's Eve 38

Farsightedness 39

The Grand Scheme 41

Hearsay 42

Max 45

Becky 46

Another One 47

All in a day 48

All moments, past, present, and future, always have existed, always will exist. 50

Good being older because I know: 52

Dead Weight 53

Letter to the Editor of The Beacon, Earth Day 1990 54

The Thinking Ocean 56

Veronica's Veil 58

Yin Yang 60

this and that 62

Minotaur 64

When you drank the world was still out there,
but for the moment it didn't have you by the throat. 66

Dear Kerry 68

At The End 71

After reading Gertrude Stein or was it Clark Coolidge 73

14 Northfield Avenue 74

High School Sweetheart 76

Time Considerations 78

At One Time 79

Clarence 81

Coat of Arms 83

Pepsi and a Package of Planters Salted Peanuts 84

Do not go gentle into that good night. 85

Fate 86

Another Quarrel

Minding my own business
reading David Markson's *This
Is Not A Novel* in bed
when for some reason looking beyond the vastness
that is my belly
I notice the lamp
hanging on the wall across the room
a dusty dull thing contrasted
against the repetitive bile-green flower pattern
leaves and sticks, begonias and whatnot
and I realize it's an ugly lamp
and I hate it

Who bought that lamp?
My wife did you blockhead, you know that

Oh yeah, guess there's nothing we can do about it then
No, nothing, you know that

Cluck, cluck, cluck
You can cluck, cluck, cluck all you damn want
but the lamp stays, I changed my mind it's a fine lamp
and shut the hell up!

Wormholes

Will he ever
be able to reverse time
return to when
he'd take her bowling or to a play
or a movie then to the diner
for tuna sandwiches and onion rings

Einstein theorized we could move forward in time
but not backwards.

They'd talk on the phone for hours
He carried her books and walked her
to her classes so the other guys knew
she was his girl

And according to Stephen Hawking:
"Any kind of time travel to the past through wormholes
or any other method is probably impossible."

A time when they dreamt of spending
their lives together never apart
until the end of time

But now string theory mathematics is postulating
that we might be able to travel backwards
through "geometric structures
called closed timelike curves" (wormholes).

He'd protect her
provide for her
entertain her
she'd know that all he cared about was her
keeping her happy and safe
never able to say no to her
doing anything and everything in his power
to make sure she was always his

The Big Bang

What if time isn't time
at all
never has been
and everything that ever happened everywhere
in the existence of the universe happened
at the exact same instant
so there was no past present or future
no beginnings middles or ends
to anything
no clocks or calendars
ticking off seconds minutes hours
days weeks months
years decades centuries . . .
no history or future prognostications
but instead
only a simple explosion of everythingness
everything ever created
time space matter energy all of it smushed
together existing together
in the selfsame moment
formed into one gigantic amorphous stew
and all that matters to any of us ever
is this moment now period.

Metaphysics

So many galaxies and solar systems careening
through the universe so many planets

Close your eyes keep still
it's a relaxation technique like counting sheep
only you're focusing on a candle's light

Many of them teeming with people and polar bears
maple trees bridges books banks bedposts
bombs brooms and bulldozers

Alone in the darkness preventing it
from flickering even a little

You wonder why life is the way it is here.
You don't really believe
the citizens, people, tentacleheads
or whatever they're called elsewhere in the universe
are paying taxes watching sit-coms smoking Marlboros
mowing lawns keeping cats goldfish canaries
listening to C&W Music while at the same time
trying incessantly to swindle rob rape kidnap explode
maim and disembowel one another just like us.

And your mind becomes
a wavelength of light searching
throughout the dark corners
of the galaxy for the beginning
of everything including sleep.

King Arthur Died in AD 538

Things are about the same
here, same as always, snowy out
another boring lunch.

Did you know that King Arthur
(of the Round Table and all that)
was real and died in 538?

Simply trying to imagine
538 is difficult, nearly impossible
so long ago, so vague and dark.

Most likely King Arthur was a Roman general

Tons of rubbish written
about the Arthurian Legends.
Like with trying to find the historical Jesus

Albert Schweitzer for example tried and failed.
But questing after the historical Arthur
could prove fruitful.

The big problem is having to learn
all those archaic languages: Saxon, Anglo,
Celtic, Kentish, Pictish, Jutish, Cumbric, Irish.

Welsh too, don't forget Welsh.
Forget it. Just getting modern English
down has kept me occupied for decades.

No, no Arthur for me.
Besides I gotta go make myself
a sandwich or something.

Ruins

Cistercian Monks inhabited Dunbrody Abbey
800 years ago
today one wonders what they thought
as they toiled on their daily chores, ceaseless
as the sun's rising in the morning
setting back down again
at the end of the day

Did they like
breaking-up the clods of thick Irish earth
or tending their flocks of sheep
or repairing the Abbey's roof and outbuildings?

Jesus, thou joy of loving hearts,
Thou fount of life, thou Light of men,
From the poor bliss that earth imparts,
We turn unfilled to thee again.

Chartered under the patronage of The Blessed Virgin Mary
by Herlewin, bishop of Leighlin
we completed our majestic Gothic Church by 1240
our farmlands were fruitful
our goats and sheep pigs and geese favored

Did they yearn to eat meat
which was forbidden them or to lay with women
forbidden them also?
Or instead were they content
with their lot in life: studying, praying, laboring

How angry were they (did they ever
get angry?) when Henry (that bastard) dissolved
this precious holy place in 1539
where to go oh where to go to begin again anew

Henry's stooges plundered the Abbey
stole everything loose toppled over the rest
finally melting down the lead roof by burning
the wood from the roof (Cannibalization! the roof
eating itself!)
rendering the place unfit for us to ever return

But at least they didn't slaughter
as Vikings would have
thanks be to the Holy Virgin's kindness

Chaste, poor, loyal, living cloistered in charity
and unconditional love and obedience
to our esteemed abbot and the Holy Roman Father.
A respectable life, perhaps yes, particularly out
on the blustery fields in the wilderness of Ireland

Nestled in the conflux of rivers Suire and Barrow
we had three vaulted chapels we did
and an enormous gothic window
dispersing God's light upon the west end portico
adorned with burnished filigree cut in stone
an extraneous embellishment tolerated by Abbot Philip
but smiled upon by all brothers lay and clerical alike

O Jesus, ever with us stay;
Make all our moments calm and bright,

Chase the dark night of sin away;
Shed o'er the world thy holy light.

But now the Abbey, its church and cloister, lay in ruins
an everlasting monument to the rigorous lives
lived there by a hardy humble few

Yes only ruins remain: craggy grass-topped walls
crooked doorways and arches opening
to empty spaces where altars once beckoned
and bare wooden tables and benches and hardened
unfeathered beds welcomed us at the end of our labors

And all this for an eternity spent in heaven
rather than in that other place

Michelangelo's David (1501-1504)

Of course you say David has been done before
but not really, not like mine
Donatello, Bellano, Verrocchio
No, David has not been done before
not by a true hand

It's as if God Himself breathed
into my block of marble
caressing him from the stone
coercing him come out alive
the sheen of his skin
the power of his rippling sinews
his determined yet calm stance
the all-knowing demeanor in his eyes
carved by the hand of God through me

But will I finish him, can I? Yes, of course
I'll finish him because I must
because I cannot leave him undone, unfinished
forever lurking within the rock
trapped half in the rock, half out
like all my unfinished pietas and slaves.
That would be blasphemy, heresy even
a half-man, half-beast creature
centaur, harpy, manticore, minotaur
furies, sirens and satyrs

My David is second only
to the real flesh and blood David

but then perhaps not even that
for the real David is dead
buried in the ground, worm food
whereas mine, mine
lives forever in space and time
not in memory only
a triumph of marble
shoulders, arms, thighs, chest, waist, back
and thighs – his thighs
are the hardest to finish

But how can you capture the movement
the power of pure perfection
isn't perfection something never to be finished?
Alas, I am lost
such a foolhardy endeavor
hubris is what it is
what I sought and seek to accomplish
is hubris, plain and simple

Who am I, a mere mortal
to chip away the marble revealing, releasing
the beauty confined within?

Where is my flagellation strap
so I can quell once again
once and for all
this indomitable hubris lurking about
in the stony darkness of my breast
hungering for release?
Hubris indeed

Perfection my ass
Who do I think I am? God. God!
Yes perhaps, perhaps
but only He knows for sure.

Gelato

"I just realized that Michelangelo's David
is the David who slays Goliath
in the Bible" says John
his face beaming.

Then David put his hand in his bag and took out a stone; and he
slung it and struck the Philistine in his forehead, so that the stone
sank into his forehead, and he fell on his face to the earth.
I Samuel 17:49

My eyes widen as I realize not everyone
on this tour of Venice, Florence and Rome
is here for the art, history and culture.
Rather than learning
about these things these people
are here to spend money on gold jewelry
leather goods, wine and Murano glass
to see olive trees and vineyards
and eat Mozzarella Fritta, Antipasto, Calamari
Gamberi Spiedo, Bruschetta, Penne al Pomodoro
Tortelloni All'aragosta, Rigatoni con Luganega
Spaghetti alla Bolognese, Porcini Agnolotti
Gnocchi di Sorrento, Pollo Parmigiano
Vitello Piccata, Panna Cotta, Torta di Formaggio
Filetto Balsamico, Mousse di Cioccolato Torta
Tiramisu, Coppa di Gelato Guarnita
topped off with an Espresso
and a glass of delicious Courvoisier Cognac.

Reality

We have not found a way to prove
absolutely what is real
in the physical world or even if it exists.
It may be only in our minds.

Had to call Jack the tree guy.
You know that giant Maple out front?
There's "sawdust" around the base, I suspect
it's infested with carpenter ants.

I shake my head at the TV.
So in 375 years we haven't progressed beyond
Descartes' *cogito ergo sum*! Unbelievable!

Since I retired I've been helping-out with our 2 grandchildren
who live right across the street, taking them
off the bus and to appointments and for frozen yogurt.

Then my wife comes in and out of the blue states:
I feel as if you've been irritated with me all day!
And I have no idea what she's talking about.
I thought we were having a really fine day
so I stand corrected reality does indeed exist only
in our minds (in some minds anyway).

No, you are not hallucinating, we are no longer Facebook Friends
I dropped from 60 "friends" down to 16 was wasting way
too much time up there voyeuring and poking around.

Blaise Pascal (1623-1662)

He often saw a bottomless void
open up along his left side
making him cling
to his chair in terror

Seek God and find the devil. That is what has happened to me.
August Strindberg (1849-1912)

Sometimes temptation forced upon him
the urge to jump
or lean over
and fall in to have done with it

We are each our own devil, and we make this world our hell.
Oscar Wilde (1854-1900)

He was desperate to find a way any way
to discover some means any means
to hide it push it
out of his reach

Hell is empty and all the devils are here.
William Shakespeare (1564-1616)

But mostly he liked it there
a reminder of what would be
if he didn't strive endlessly
to find meaning in life

Hell is empty and all the devils are here.

William Shakespeare (1564-1616)
The Tempest, Act 1, Scene 2

Crossroads
Could've traded my soul
to the Devil for poetic perfection
that time I met him at the crossroads
but chose the girl instead

Kerry
Renal carcinoma spreading rapidly. What can I do? "Nothing.
He just wants to get it over with as soon as possible"
the Devil hisses in my ear.

Big John
Photo on his 70th BD
no longer the toughest guy
gaunt and gray now, fighting to keep
the Devil from pulling him under

Olympians
Watching the Olympic champions thinking
I could've done that if only I had the resources . . .
then spot the Devil across the room laughing his ass off

Poetry
Countless hours
submitting poems to journals
and for what? The Devil shrugs.
"Don't look at me.
Warned you for years
you're wasting your time."

Wife
If she stops loving you she won't warn you or discuss it.
She'll simply send you packing and there's nothing
you can do about it, hisses the Devil.

Existentialism

I'm just saying, we think we can develop and improve
ourselves personally, intellectually, physically,
emotionally, but isn't it all a lie
or rather a pack of lies?

Donald, such a coincidence, just last night I read a poem
about Edvard Munch written back in 1958 by John Wieners
an old Beat poet, I think you'll love it

We always want to appear to be better
smarter, sharper, more perfect, stronger, faster
more unflappable and worldly-wise
than we are. But really, can we? Can we really?

Remember that time George shot a pea from
his peashooter at the old dresser in the basement
and the thing fell right over with a bang and some dust

What you see is what you get.
Be stoic, existential even and accept what is
rather than always trying to prove
what might be, knowing of course it can't be.

Fate is immutable don't you get it.
Change anathema. So relax have a beer
watch the ball game on TV accept yourself
as you are stop whimpering and shut the fuck up!

Swarm Bots

Machinus examinis

What is life you ask?
Seriously, still this same old question?
I wish you people weren't so damned uncertain
of yourselves and your place in the universe.

Am I life a tiny robotic ant
a construction of metal plastic rubber
and computer chips skittering all over the place
under my own power mind you
bleeping blinking humming and chirping
communicating with my fellow bots
electronically (telepathically some would say)
rather than chemically (so old-fashioned)
or verbally so what's the difference really?

According to the *Future and Emerging Technologies
Program* of the *European Commission* (IST-2000-31010)
we Swarm Bots are self-organizing
and self-assembling artifacts
coordinated multirobotic systems
capable of collective behavior and swarm intelligence, i.e. –
I move under my own volition
I communicate with others of my own and other species (you)
I feel my surroundings, learn to respond to stimuli
and to quote one of our hero humans
I think therefore I am. To put it simply so you humans
won't be confused and stuck

in your normal mode of equivocation –
I am alive because I say so. Period.

Higgs Boson

Physicists call it the God Particle
because they believe it is the foundation
for all the other particles
making everything in the Universe
indeed the Universe itself
possible

Green grass, azure skies, orange foothills,
red seas and dead seas and sunsets
purple mountains majesty

4 July 2012 the auditorium is full
all the luminaries of physics astrophysics astronomy cosmology
the Higgs hunters all gathered for the announcement

CERN's Large Hadron Collider propels two high-energy protons
to smash into each other at the speed of light (almost)
splattering their innards all over the place

10 billion dollars and 10 years later
the largest single machine in the history of the world
well worth it the feeling in the room unanimous

The Higgs Boson is too minuscule to be detected outright
but it must be there for the mathematics says so

$$\mathcal{L}_H = \left| \left(\partial_\mu - igW_\mu^a \tau^a - i\frac{g'}{2}B_\mu \right) \phi \right|^2 + \mu^2\phi^\dagger\phi - \lambda(\phi^\dagger\phi)^2,$$

we look instead for the particle byproducts produced
from its disintegration
within a trillionth of a second

Quarks, photons, muons, gluons, gravitons, neutrinos
leptons, majorons, squarks, branons, dilatons
mesons, zinos, winos, gluinos . . .

But now what else is there
to be discovered seeing as you've explained
how everything in the Universe works

On the day of the great announcement, a Wednesday
Peter Higgs himself 40 years after his initial prediction
in the front row, eyes tearing
throat too constricted to say much except
"I never expected this to happen in my lifetime"

The 2013 Nobel Prize for Physics, Higgs
along with François Englert:
"for the theoretical discovery of a mechanism that contributes to
our understanding of the origin of mass of subatomic particles, and
which recently was confirmed through the discovery of the
predicted fundamental particle"

My Lord, My Sweet Lord

So now what? What else is there? Is physics all done?
Don't be silly it's on to proving
the Super Symmetry Math Model by finding sparticles
(no, not Spartacus, pay attention)
after all, there is no end to infinity.

From Nothing

Physicists, astrophysicists, geophysicists, astrobiologists,
astronomers, cosmologists . . . all of them
state it like it's clear, obvious,
irrefutable – in the beginning
of the universe there was nothing, nothing at all,
no space, no time, no matter, no energy, only emptiness.
Then suddenly out of the darkness
out of nowhere for no reason
like someone flipping a switch
an infinitesimally small speck of something-or-other
appeared then immediately exploded
into the Big Bang BOOM!!!
And the universe – everything there is
or was or ever shall be –
spiral galaxies, dwarf stars, planets, comets, asteroids,
black holes, quasars, quarks, dark matter, neutrinos,
gravitons, photons, mesons, and the Higgs Boson –
was formed just like that, from nothing,
absolutely nothing.
Seriously?

Moonlight

Just look at it
high, full, bright
shifting the shapes of trees
across the lawn

At first I thought the moon
was a UFO hanging in the night sky,
get out of the car stare up at it,
look around for someone
to tell, but no
it's only the moon you moron.

There's even a paperclip shining
on the sidewalk
as golden light descends
through a tangle of branches
to glisten on the cold metal benches

Her form in the moonlight
pure, sure, undeniable
casting a mellow shadow across the sheets

After turning off the sprinklers
we would lie on our backs
on the 18th green
looking up at Draco, Orion, Gemini

But mostly I hid in the bushes
staring up at her room
hoping for a glimpse

History of Midnight

After finishing his watering duties
he's lying on his back
on the seventh green looking up
at Orion and Gemini and Taurus the Bull

We like to think if given the chance
to go back to the very beginning
things might be different
the second time around
we wouldn't make the same mistakes again
we could do things right this time
we wouldn't behave like an ass
insensitive, hurting people
disappointing them, making them cry

Amazed that the Greeks and Sumerians
could pick out those arrangements
in the vast jumble of stars overhead

Fixing it so she doesn't dump you
for some other guy who doesn't come close
to deserving a girl like her (any more than you do)
doesn't return your calls
telling you with a phony frown
that you're moving too fast for her
she needs her freedom
to experience other guys

He's even more amazed
when his girl lies down beside him
pressing herself against him
as they stare at the heavens
hoping the future will reveal
that order and beauty for them too

Yes we like to think
if given a second chance
we could get it right
but history has proven
it doesn't work that way

Can't Find You

Frantically, not at first but after
a while, I'm searching everywhere
throughout the giant sprawling house
we're in for a celebration of something or other
giant dark and shadowy, stuffy, no windows
no sunlight so many rooms and corridors
narrow up and down

Trying out for the Senior Class Play's romantic lead opposite my
girl but coming in second to the ever-popular handsome hunky
Everett then having to watch him romancing her on-stage from
backstage for weeks.

People sprawled everywhere
some sleeping or sitting or standing staring
leaning against walls and closet doors
talking in whispers, nonchalantly,
but no one noticing me
as I search for you going through
the rooms and corridors one by one

I take the train to my girlfriend's school to surprise her during
finals. She sits, quiet, not looking at me, one pretty leg folded
under, finally blurting, "You have to leave. I have a date today
with another guy." Never saw that one coming, nope, not after
being together 3 years already.

I search everywhere then come back around
do it all over again

like checking the same pocket 100 times
for a missing key
so damn dark, strange faces and masks
no one talking to me acknowledging me
as if I'm a ghost

Before leaving campus I find an upper window in the cafeteria,
watch her in her new winter coat with the fluffy collar, playful and
giggling, romping in the snow, throwing little snowballs at her new
beau, her lustrous brown hair shining in the sun.

Where have you gone my love
my job has always been to protect you
I am lost and forlorn, feeling more and more
hopeless checking every corner
behind every curtain, every door
on every staircase and chair
in the kitchen and bathrooms, closets

Working 3 jobs my last summer in college to buy a diamond ring
my girl would be proud to wear before she got tempted by the
wealthy football hero who'd begun following her around and
"studying" with her.

But perhaps you've left without me?
My time with you was up I always knew . . .
no, no, I'll go round again and again
you have to be here somewhere
you have to be.

She's your wife but she's not really yours. If she stops loving you
she won't warn you or tolerate a discussion about it, it'll simply
happen and she'll send you packing and there's nothing, not thing
one, you can do about it, hisses the Devil in my ear.

What If?

What if dad hadn't died when I was only 15?
I'd have him to talk to today
He'd probably be proud of me
What if I never moved out of suburban New Jersey?
I'd still be there, same old same old
Could visit my dad's and brother's grave routinely
What if my first girlfriend never dumped me?
We'd have broken up anyway when she moved away
What if I kept up my saxophone or guitar lessons?
Proof that music is my true passion
What if I never left that day you sent me away?
Proof I had balls
But you would've been angry at me
What if I made it into Veterinary school?
Would've spent my life doing something useful
What if I were a man for once standing my ground?
I'd be a true alpha-male
But you would've been angry at me
What if I had earned my black belt in Karate?
I would've smashed Big Don your favorite study-buddy
right in his fucking head
What if your big blind date turned out to be great?
I wouldn't be here right now
What if I finished my PhD in Comparative Literature?
I'd be a professor somewhere, able to speak other languages
What if I made you choose between him and me?
I'd be married to some other girl
Or maybe never married at all
What if texting had existed back in the sixties?

I would've lost you for sure
Out-texted by some hunky dude on your campus
What if you belonged to another man, were another man's wife?
I would've come after you anyway
What if time isn't time and never has been?
That's a tough one

New Year's Eve

Just another New Year's Eve like 50 others we've had together but I feel like asking her if she's happy she married me such a beauty she could've had any guy she wanted and here she is still with me doing nothing on New Year's Eve except watching TV. But it is only three damn degrees outside. We can't take that ball-dropping-in-Time's-Square-nonsense anymore, nothing but commercials unwatchable really so we watched Jurassic Park III and a Doc Martin and a New Girl always good to end the evening (and the year) with something lighthearted and funny. And we had popcorn seeing as we are both on diets have a few more pounds to lose. I didn't ask her if she's glad she married me I think she is. My world revolves around her and I am attentive (and protective and possessive and jealous) as hell but asking those kinds of questions is foolhardy business. I did tell her I love everything about her and she said yes I know so that's something. She hates the romantic stuff always gives me a hard time about it. But the moon's out there high and full a bright beacon of optimism in the darkness etching the shadows of the winter trees across the snowy lawn romantic as hell whether she likes it or not HA!

Farsightedness

Forgot my eyeglasses again
that guy looks like Cary Grant or Uncle Johnny
before he got sick with Lou Gehrig's disease.

Rhubarb pies? Nobody eats rhubarb pies!

I fooled Todd he thought
I was playing amazing harmonica
it was so silly too many beers was all.

Almost forgot to feed the fucking fish again (in my dream).

The bus took forever going up Madison.
Alan was getting antsy and angry
but I didn't mind it was fun looking at the people.

George and I would walk Hartz Lane past all the junk yards
all the way to 2 Guys From Harrison.

Think it's going to rain again tomorrow? Hope not, I want to
swim.

Drive-in movies were great weren't they?
One time we snuck Pat and Larry in in the trunk of the car.

Johnny was so crazy about Lois he had photos
of her taped to the dash of his new GTO.

I was jealous when she'd dance with Dick

he had such long arms and couldn't stop staring at her.

That guy shouldn't be allowed to touch her, let alone dance with
her, she's a goddess!

Doc Johnson took us up once in his airplane
Pat got sick such a drab day for photographs
like channeling ghosts the doc said

In the Staten Island Zoo the sun bear paced
back and forth in perpetuum
flamingos a 2-headed turtle and otters

Camels really are ugly beasts! So are Yaks!

Keep your hands off her she's my girl I stated matter-of-factly
and he did, of course he did I was a weightlifter.

Not sure how I survived high school and college without losing
her.
What is such a beautiful girl doing with you, the guys would ask.

Hyperopia is the medical term for farsightedness
whereby distant objects
are seen clearly close objects are not.

The Grand Scheme

Sounds as if you follow life where it takes you
I guess we all do that one
way or another (oftentimes kicking and screaming)

A stitch in time saves nine.

thinking about this just yesterday
how you take a job and it pulls you in one direction
meet people, find a girl, and you are off in another direction

A rolling stone gathers no moss.

get a promotion, move to a new city . . .
before you know it you are living across the street
from your daughter and her husband and their 2 children

Don't count your chickens before they're hatched.

going to the grandson's basketball games,
the granddaughter's softball games and school plays,
McDonald's and swimming in Walden Pond and . . .

If I've told you once I've told you 1000 times.

suddenly where in the fuck did 70 years go
and I hope I get to see Paris and Bob Dylan one more time
before I shuffle off my mortal coil

Hearsay

"It's just pain," my doctor friend Eddie said when I told him my back was killing me.

"I'm not good at self-discipline and setting goals like you are," my brother said as he took another sip of his vodka tonic.

"My answer is yes that is if you still want me to be your girl." I almost passed out.

"Good thing college boy you're not trying to make your living out here, on this here road crew." And he's laughing and swinging his shovel like a golf club.

"I'd pay $1000 a roll to get the hell out of this store right now," he exclaims as his wife pulls another book off the rack.

"You're in that season of your life, need to develop a conservative portfolio," advises Danielle my pretty young financial advisor.

"She's out of my league," many friends have told me over the years, indicating really that she's out of my league too.

"Nobody buys CDs anymore. All the music you could possibly want is now right here." He's wiggling the stupid iPhone at me.

Her hair pure white moussed sticking straight up down the middle of her head. "After I almost died of cancer I said fuck it."

Losing her memory faster now didn't even recognize me when I said, "Aunt Jean it's me, Choo-Choo!"

Joe, retired now at home, sick with congestive heart failure, sick of feeling useless. "I'm getting a job pumping gas," he asserts to his wife.

After Joe died, Linda began dating again. "No, of course Peter won't be sitting in daddy's old chair," she tells her daughter."

Backing track star Donnie into a corner advising him to "keep your fucking hands off her and stop sending her notes in class she's my girl you idiot!"

He never leaves his tiny art studio. "If not for this wheelchair I'd be in a nursing home," he states sending shivers through me.

"Guess what I found in my junk drawer where I keep the clutter I don't know what to do with – that book of poems you wrote." Swell Mom, that's swell.

"Don't recall why I dumped you," she wrote. "So stupid of me. I realize now that you were the love of my life." Oh boo-hoo he thought, serves you right.

All she kept saying was: "Damn raccoon was trapped in my bathroom, tore the rubber plunger to shreds!"

Surprised how pretty Aunt Dottie was in her wedding photo taken 70 years ago. "She's not pretty," my wife declares. "She's young."

He doesn't comprehend "friends with benefits." "If my girl had a "friend" who enjoyed her "benefits" he'd be dead and I'd be in jail – simple as that.

Married 63 years when he entered assisted-living, lost his freedom and most of his memory. "Have I ever been married," he asked.

On the TSA line I recognize Josh Charles. I touch his arm. "You were on The Good Wife." He nods, "Yeah" and turns away.

"There are so many other incredible things besides your wife's beauty to write about," Larry, my poetry mentor insists. Really?

Don't get the point of climbing Mt. Everest all the while obsessing about not falling off just so you can spend 3 minutes at the top saying "Oh look how pretty."

Up again at 3 a.m. grabbing my pad and pen, the Muse nudging me, hissing in my ear, "Come on man move it I got things to say."

Max

He's protecting the homestead barking
and lunging at the lawnmower guy
on the other side of the window
a product of man's domestication
for protection, companionship.

Shall we grill tonight dear
or get Chinese take-out or Mexican?

Doesn't matter to me.
Did you see on the news
more pilot whales beached themselves
near Judique on Cape Breton?
Wonder why they do that.

No one knows why. Could be confusion
caused by sonar
or fear of shark attacks or from poison
or pollution or something in the weather
who knows?

Max for crying out loud stop barking! Quiet!

Chinese it is.
Does Max know they eat dogs in China?

Becky

If Becky got out she'd make a beeline
to the Shop-N-Bag in the center of town
let herself in through
the automatic door
head straight to the meat counter
help herself to chicken cutlets
or beef kebabs. Easy for her to reach
being a large St. Bernard.
Burt the store manager would call Herb
madder than a wet hen,
"Come get this damn dog Pronto!"
But never was Burt as upset as Herb was
that night Becky
gave birth to 10 pups
one of which came out deformed.
Herb held the quivering lump in his hands
cried and cried
buried it out behind the barn.

Another One

The latest high school news
going around is Mike R– died.
Did you hear that?

No. What happened to him?

I tried a few searches, but found nothing
about his death. Only that he and Celia
were lawyers in Philadelphia.

She has a Facebook page
but it's not on there, only their picture.
God she's still beautiful!
But I would never have recognized him
and there's no obit.

Celia was our football queen you recall.
I never said one word to her back then.
She was one of those untouchable beauties,
terrifying guys like us.
I had hard enough time talking
to my own girlfriend for crying out loud.

I never talked to her either. Like that
commercial says: She's out of your network.

Hard to believe 50 years have gone by.
But some things do remain timeless
and unchanging – like her beauty.

All in a day

At times this house seems so big too big especially
since the children moved out.

My mother called to tell me Remy
has prostate cancer which got me alarmed
so I call Sandy, his wife, my cousin.

Perhaps we should downsize seeing as we only use
half the rooms. All we really need are
the bedroom and TV room, kitchen, bath, dining room,
Patti's office and my library, and the laundry room.

So Sandy called me back while we were in
T.J. Maxx not shopping really
but there for a walk. Have cabin fever
and really needed to walk but the freezing rain
and fog drove us indoors.

3 to 4 other rooms we don't need.
We should really find another place altogether
downsize properly. But two of our grandchildren
live right across the street (118 steps door-to-door)
so Patti isn't going anywhere
therefore neither am I.

Sandy told me because the cancer
was minimal they would use radiation
on his prostate not surgery.

The docs had been watching it for some time now.
That was very good to hear.

Then after dinner Jesse called.
An old high school friend we recently
reconnected with. No agenda he said just felt
like talking with you, with an old friend.
So that was a nice ending to a hectic and fretful day.

All moments, past, present, and future, always have existed, always will exist.

Kurt Vonnegut, Jr. (1922-2007)

Time Travel
I'd love to travel back
see dinosaurs, meet Jesus
Mozart, Shakespeare.
But have no interest in revisiting
moments in my life
when I behaved badly.

Carpe Diem
How can you accept the infirmities that overtake us?
How can you be at peace with a shrinking future,
living more in the past, watching
family and friends disappear one by one?

Mistakes
Imagine how grand it will be
when physicists unravel the key to time travel
and you can go back and fix
your big mistakes before
they happen.

Time
If you could slow down time from going so fast
would you? Or let it continue dragging you closer
and closer
to the end every day.

Nostalgia

When will astrophysicists reverse time sending me back
to our beginning among those perfect moments with her
where I long to return to be alive once again.

Good being older because I know:

when to call the plumber and when I can fix it myself (most
times)
we no longer need a bigger house, a faster car
there are no more corporate ladders to climb
I don't have to worry about impressing self-serving bosses
and idiot co-workers
getting angry over political machinations is fruitless
not to get into a tizzy over unwanted marketing calls
I don't become offended as easily as I once did
like when store clerks call me sir
I don't have to laugh at jokes that aren't funny
what I'm good at and not
when I'm tired I can nap
don't always have to be right
music is the nectar of the gods
I can't win every argument
I don't have to pretend to like football and golf, salsa and beer
don't have to paint the entire house over one weekend
fantasizing about sex is a dead-end road
memories become stronger and more important especially
when they involve my girl, my childhood sweetheart
I still feel guilty if I have a slice of pie or a bowl of ice cream
but it doesn't stop me.

Dead Weight

Just spoke with mom.
She just had lunch with Kathleen.
Todd is going there I think she said tomorrow
then on Thursday off to the airport
and on to Cape May for Dana's graduation.

They will be staying in Atlantic City
as there are no hotels available on Cape May.
Her back is giving her fits
but she has to do this because of
her beloved granddaughter.

Told her she should arrange a wheelchair
they had some discussion about that.
Hope it works out.
I asked if Roberta was going and she said no,
she has business. I asked if Athena
was going and she said yes
but not with them.

She wouldn't know what to say to her.
I told her she should probably say hello,
how are you, nice to see you, blah, blah, blah.
Amazing how all this dead weight
is carried forward.

Letter to the Editor of *The Beacon*, Earth Day 1990

from Laura, Katie, Stephanie and Kathleen, all age 13

Railroad Pond: old rug, tin foil, sign post,
rusted bucket, bucket of gasoline, old shirt,
curlers, tire, screen, sewage leak, old stove,
beer can, rusty ironing board, cement blocks

"We are 4 students at the R. J. Grey Junior High who are concerned about our environment."

K-Mart Pond: 12 metal shopping carts, barrels,
cardboard sheets, rags, foam pieces, plant pot,
gasoline container, cigarette package, 5 tires,
candy wrappers, rusty basins, strips of rubber,
plastic bags, plastic crate, 9 plastic bottles

"We think that it is polluted and us kids are going to be the ones affected by all this pollution in the future."

High School Pond: wooden bench, newspapers,
beer bottles, rusted pipe, truck tire, bags,
plastic foam containers, wrappers and boxes,
wheels, plastic pail, plastic tubes, cement

"So far we have examined 4 local ponds and we have found that they are very polluted."

Flagg Hill Pond: deflated boat, Pepsi bottle,
potato chip bags, metal container, waste pipe,
newspaper, plastic foam, coffee cups, a metal
table, a dead fish and some bubbly orange scum

"We were wondering what the adults were going to do about it
besides tell us kids to adopt a stream."
(Earth Day 1990)

The Thinking Ocean

Why not? Who's to say
the ocean isn't a super-organism
composed of multitudes of lesser organisms
like the Amazon rainforest, the Insect Kingdom,
the Milky Way?

The ocean is a sentient thinking being
circulating itself all around the globe
currents are its heartbeats
bacteria its immune system
swells and tides its musculature.
It has a metabolism.
It eats, breathes, recycles nutrients
through its estuaries and river mouths.

Mother Ocean, Tethys, Yemaya, Amphitrite . . .

Bacterial nanowires form her nervous system,
a neural-net patchwork below
in her sediments, spreading
throughout the abyssal valleys
and mountain ranges,
equivalent to our own
cerebral cortex.

What does she feel
as whales scream in their death throes?

What does she think
as oil-spill pollutants suffocate clam beds and bird nests?

What can she do
as garbage and marine debris choke her shores?

And what will she decide, how will she REACT—
being more mighty and powerful
than any human endeavor—
in order to protect herself
and the creatures alive within her?

She is the greatest of super-organisms.
She can, if she chooses, once again swallow
EVERYTHING—
all of us on the planet
as she did in the time of Noah.

Veronica's Veil

First thing in the morning waiting
in the Dental Implants & Periodontics office
can't hear my wife back there
only some typical drilling and grinding noises

Thinking of my buddy Herbie
how he always has something friendly
to say to everyone he meets
a kindly comment, an insightful question
something outrageous in the news

Now it's quiet back there
this orthodontist never talks
to her patients has the personality
of an old boot

Unlike Herbie Mr. People-Person Extraordinaire
like he's always running for mayor
fun being around him really
most of the time

Now there's some contraption rattling
around back there the amalgamator probably
mixing up some amalgam

Last night we watched an unexpectedly engaging
documentary on TV about the Veil of Veronica
something I never knew about
and I'm a Renaissance man

Endodontics, implantology, periodontology
prosthodontics, orthodontics . . .
why are these offices always so empty?

Veronica represents the sixth station
of the cross she wiped the sweat and blood
off Christ's face with her veil
as he stumbled on his way to Calvary

Oh I hear my wife laughing that's good

These days Herbie spends most of his time
looking after his birds and rabbits, grandchildren
lopsided barn and new pergola entwined with wisteria
and worrying about money
because he's retired on a fixed income

The image of Christ's face on Veronica's Veil
clear as day, beautiful, a true miracle
but modern research has determined the veil
is not a veil at all but the burial cloth
covering Christ's face as he lay in his tomb

She's almost done back there
they're shuffling around rinsing finishing up

St. Veronica is never mentioned in the Bible
her name actually began as Vera Icon (Veronica)
meaning true image in Latin and Greek
the veil depicting the accurate image
of the resurrected Christ's face
although it turns out St. Veronica herself
never existed at all

Yin Yang

I'm fine looking after the grandchildren
all day long while you all work

WTF! I lose another entire day babysitting!

Hey you two rascals we can't watch TV all day
how 'bout we play Sorry or Uno, Battleship or Operation

Have you no shame you insincere bastard
you loathe board games!

OK kids time for lunch
Mac & Cheese, hot dogs or nice fluffy omelets?

Gag me with a spoon you hypocritical moron
you don't even cook lunch for yourself.

What flavor frozen yogurt did you two get?
Strawberry crème, Oreo cookie dough . . .

Frozen yogurt again! For crying out loud
you hate frozen fucking yogurt
where's the real ice cream?

Oh lookie at all the beautiful butterflies flying around –
yellow, blue, red . . . The Butterfly Place
is the most tranquil refuge on the planet

I hope this fucking place burns down
I really do, frying all the stupid worms with wings
blurts the Devil perched
like usual on my shoulder

this and that

She cannot walk around the yard without pulling weeds.

The cable technician arranged orange cones around his truck and ladder.

No, heights don't bother me except for being on those glass bottom elevators and platforms.

Birds are building a nest on the lighting fixture above our front door. Can't tell what they are.

Spaghetti and meatballs would be great, need the carbs after my workout.

Mostly old women in the doctor's office on Tuesday afternoon with their canes walkers and wheelchairs.

Labs came back: eosinophils high, testosterone low, but all in all not bad.

Strong as an ox, healthy as a horse, stubborn as a mule!

Have them check your Vitamin D levels, always low in old people living in New England.

Best to discourage the birds from building a nest right there, we use that door constantly.

I do hate going to the doctor's always feel so old sitting there with all the others with their walkers and canes.

But still the weeds thrive, and the crabgrass too by the way. Not using that lawn service again next year. I can grow crabgrass and weeds just fine all by myself.

Minotaur

Asterion minotaurus

I'm the victim do you hear me!
I'm the fucking victim here!
My mother Pasiphaë satisfying her unquenchable lust
(damn Aphrodite) by copulating with a bull – a damn BULL!
Who does that, seriously WHO!
My mother the great WHORE that's who
and what am I supposed to do with that image
where am I supposed to put it?
how do I deal with it psychologically? Well HOW?

So of course I'm born a hideous monster
a slaveringly insane ferocious half-man half-beast
with horns and all, scared the bejesus outta everybody
I can tell you that, was kinda funny, the look on their faces.
So King Minos my sensitive and selfless stepdad
brings in Daedalus the Crafty
who constructs a vast maze
beneath Knossos Palace as my prison
to ensure that my life remained forever a living hell.

Well of course I ate people
it was an age of human sacrifice for crying out loud!
I loved those succulent virgin girls and boys
sacrificed to me every few years.
What else would you have me do stuck alone
in that damnable endless labyrinth
until Ariadne with her stupid ball of twine

lead the great hero Theseus ooohhh aaahhh
to the heart of the matter where he . . .

Yes and then there was Theseus
Theseus the Great, the King, the Conqueror, the Coward!
The perfidious little prick snuck up on me in the dark
speared me in the face. The Bastard!
How was I supposed to know he was there
no one was ever there NO ONE! EVER! BUT! HA!
I get the final laugh because I live on yes I do
I live on immortal as the beast within you within Everyman
and shall so remain until the end of days.

When you drank the world was still out there, but for the moment it didn't have you by the throat.

Charles Bukowski (1920-1994)

Merlot

Received note after sending him *Under the Volcano*
best novel on alcoholism. "Reading every day out on the patio
with a nice bottle of Merlot."

Vodka

Determined to drink himself to death and after a year
of daily Vodka swilling became so sick he almost did die.
Cured his drinking for good.

Scotch

Never seen anyone so drunk up till 3 AM yelling
in the hallway almost getting us kicked out of the hotel
the night before our son's wedding.

Brandy

Fifty years old living with his parents
ever since he lost his license, job, son and wife
almost his life. But still he will not stop drinking.

Rum

Cousin Tommy died today drank himself to death finally
after years of trying. Such a shame though,
wasting a life.

Gin

I knew he had a serious drinking problem when he called
to confess he slept with his best friend's wife
and all these years I thought he was gay.

Dear Kerry

Didn't mean to pester you over the weekend
but I was worried because you didn't call me on my birthday
like you usually do

Male lions will kill cubs sired by other males
if they catch them but they don't eat them

So I was just checking to see if you were all right
I realize you're in your "reclusive" phase
avoiding people, staying in with the curtains closed

Bats have colonized every continent except Antarctica
crowding beneath bridges, into attics, caves, and belfries

As a recovering alcoholic
being alone all the time is a recipe for disaster
don't forget your brush with death

Female Pine Processionary Moths live only one day enough time
to fly to a new tree have sex lay 200 eggs and die (of exhaustion)

Todd and Philip came over and I flew down
from Boston and we cleaned your house
there were even flies in your refrigerator!

The Outback's nomadic pelican flocks fly,
migrate and hunt together soaring on thermal winds

We removed 56 empty vodka bottles (the 2 liter ones)
and got you to the hospital, where you almost died.
Dude, what's it gonna take?

Super Crocs grew 40 feet long 8 tons of terror attacking
and killing even the mighty dinosaurs

I was so proud of you when you recovered
took up the piano again, learned the violin,
joined a church, sang in the choir

Devilfish they are called today but the ancients knew them
and their Giant Squid cousins as The Kraken

But now you're up to your old tricks again,
not answering the phone, not calling your mother
it is so fucking tedious

Imagine if you dare a creature nine feet tall nine feet long
500 pounds, razor talons, a giant hooked beak – The Terror Bird

All you do is go to work come home
watch TV alone in the dark
dude, that's gotta make you crazy

Giant Huntsman Spiders big as dinner plates with long hairy
crab-like legs are the largest spiders in the world

When are you going to get that through your thick head
you can't be solitary and stay off the sauce
it just doesn't work that way

Since before the Dark Ages we have been lurking beneath
the freezing deep dark waters of Loch Ness

Well okay that's it for now
take care of yourself
we miss you and we love you

Hyenas are vicious hunters bringing down
zebras, giraffes and wildebeests laughing all the while

Love, Your Brother

At The End

After *The Scream* painted by Edvard Munch

A man trapped
in nature
confused out of sync with nature.

Don't know what to say to my brothers
hanging around wringing their hands waiting
for me to die

Hallucinating in coiling colors dark and bold
as he's being bent and torn
by nature coming undone.

The disease is overwhelming me
pain and exhaustion making me weaker
feeling so isolated helpless hapless hopeless
so alone not knowing how to get out of this mess

Is he screaming or about to scream?
Has he any recourse, anywhere to go?

But I have more life left to live I shout
at the gods shaking my fist at the dirty bastards

He has no control
is captured and contorted by
his environment, with nature herself
just as the Romantics wanted to be
at the start of the Industrial Revolution.

And they came Katie and Emily with their guitars
and mandolins their long dark hair and tight jeans
and played *Angel from Montgomery*
keeping me alive for two more days
those dear sweet girls I miss them already

After reading Gertrude Stein or was it Clark Coolidge

Across the room a child's rocking chair still life in the sunlight to the pigeon coop out back out in the back yard from which Mike and Venus the pigeons would take flight when Dad that scamp would point the garden hose from the back yard through the basement window at me on the inside slyly as if fixing the old Buick in the driveway by sorting nuts and bolts would somehow be beneficial in some way any way but smell the coffee percolating on the stove all the way into the back bedroom shared by my brother and me with the picture of Jesus hanging in the closet collection of empty yogurt cups stacked behind the door the hamster cages the saxophone in its case if only it could play its own damn self such an embarrassment like the crumbling curb out front the weeds and that time the giant spider with the hairy legs startled mom in her bedroom after dad died and she screamed out and those ubiquitous shiny black water beetles always scurrying beneath everything in the basement: the Army rations barbells bookshelves washing machine tool bench while upstairs on the wall in the hall the phone rang and rang but nobody heard except Kerry but he didn't answer because he hated that place and was gone by then anyway.

14 Northfield Avenue

I'm back again
in the Northfield Avenue house
the one we were raised in
in suburban New Jersey
a typical, post-World War II development
across from Old Smith's Orchard and Farm

Don't recall ever seeing my father cry, only my grandfather who
wept after his son died.

noises outside I peer peepishly out
see a car parked on the lawn. . . the LAWN!
an old Chevy
then sense dark figures slouching
along the walls of the house

ever wonder how many people from the early
days still live on the old block? The Gordons, Wilsons,
Hanleys, Tighes, Violas, Watts, Crawfords . . .

I rush to the doors and windows
making certain they're bolted and latched
close the blinds
no one can see into the living room
dining room kitchen Kerry's bedroom

Of course I can't paint the whole house anymore took me a day
just to do the windowsills.

I find him upstairs in his room in the far corner at his desk
so absorbed in writing something he doesn't see
or hear me and I can't get his attention

back downstairs so dark I feel along the wall
searching for the light switch
in our old dining room
but can't find it

Enthralled in my youth by The Catcher in the Rye and Of Human
Bondage and The Fountainhead, all unreadable for me now.

notice my girlfriend in a corner
slivers of moonlight all around her
arms folded
that scowl of disapproval
tugging at her mouth

Just because you were friends in high school 40 years ago doesn't
mean you'll be friends until the day you die.

perhaps it isn't as bad out there
as I first thought

High School Sweetheart

- **Love**
- **Perseverance**
- **Romance**

Love

Looking up at me holding my hand tightly in the cool
afternoon sunlight at the football game: *We are the Bears
the Mighty Mighty Bears* . . . telling me "Yes I will go steady
with you I will be your girl if you still want me."

Not sure how I survived high school without losing her. What is
such a beautiful girl doing with you, the guys would ask.

Imprint precious moments of your life on your soul so they never
leave you in this life or the next.

We are never so defenseless against suffering as when we love.
Sigmund Freud (1856-1939)

Perseverance

Not going away as perhaps I should have after she
returned my "going steady" ring to me after only 2 weeks –
when you have to have her you have to have her so you hold on
for dear life all your life – simple as that.

Boys who had girlfriends didn't usually have the time for much else. They were too busy guarding what they thought was theirs.

Life can knock the stuffing out of you especially if you spend your time worrying about love or money.

If a man finds the thing he wants, he holds it steadfastly.
William IX (1071-1127)

Romance

Holding my breath leaning over to steal my first kiss nearly
missing her mouth in the darkened spotlight booth
of the high school auditorium during
a rehearsal of "The Sound of Music" but a kiss is a kiss.

No matter how we tried to avoid him, Mr. Pinfield always man-
aged to catch young lovers holding hands in the hallways.

Do what you love FIRST! Do all the nuts and bolts stuff later,
whenever. It's only filler anyway.

And if her lips had stayed much longer against mine,
she would have sucked out my soul, when I kissed her.
Clement Marot (1496-1544)

Time Considerations

Can all this be true
all this that's happening?
After all these years
can you return to the beginning
as if the in-between
simply never existed?

You can't go home again
Thomas Wolfe said
but where is home anyway
and what did he know
he was a novelist not a poet.

But do you really want to go back
do you think you could fix anything
by going back
avoid your stupid little personal disasters
your bitter embarrassments?
Do you think history won't
repeat itself for once?

Do you think the girls
would treat you differently
or the boys think you fit and strong
a worthy opponent
giving you a wide berth?
No it would all happen all over again
same things
only this time maybe worse.

At One Time

I was very interested
in Astronomy
knew all about the planets
and their moons
the types and distances of stars
about comets
and meteors, asteroids
black holes and supernovae.

The universe includes all matter found in galaxies and in intergalactic space: atomic particles followed by atoms, molecules, dust, space rocks, comets, asteroids, moons, dwarf planets, planets, solar systems, stars, black holes, nebulae, galaxies, dark energy and dark matter. (According to BioEd Online).

At one time I
could lie on my back
on a grassy hill
at night
and point out
Ursa Minor, Orion
the Hunter, Taurus
the Bull and all
the rest of the pantheon.

The Sun is just one of over 100 billion stars in our Milky Way Galaxy, and the Milky Way is just one of over 100 billion galaxies in the known universe which equals:

1,000,000,000,000,000,000,000,000 or a "1" with 24 zeros after it –
1 septillion stars. Only a rough number, however.

But now I never
can get to it. Life
has snagged me by the toe
so many other things to do
so many other things
in the way.

I miss it. I really do miss it.

Clarence

Do you think losing a loved one makes you stronger?

The plumbers two of them here for hours
trying to clear the kitchen drain:
snakes plungers Shop-Vacs . . .
and still the damn drain remains clogged.

Dad's death made me stronger. I was 15 became
the man of the house had to be stronger.

Greg says to Dave go downstairs
check if the water is flowing
by listening at the Estabrook. Wait what?
Did I hear him correctly? The Estabrook?

In the morning we went to a band concert of fifth and sixth
graders. Our grandson plays the clarinet: This Old Man.

But to lose a brother when you're both in your 60s doesn't
do a goddamn bit of good for anyone
no matter how you rationalize it.

Estabrook? That's my name. Greg's brow furrows.
It's a standard pipe fitting collects multiple drainlines.
Yes still used today.
Estabrooks are all over the place. Wow. I never knew.

I played clarinet too and sax when I was a youngster
all the way through high school
didn't like it much didn't practice much either.

Anyway, we finally had to call Roto-Rooter Plumbing
& Water Cleanup, cleared it in 10 minutes.

For the demon cancer to cut you down destroy your life
in an avalanche of pain and suffering proves
only one thing: there's no God anywhere
no benevolent God that is.

Should've kept up playing sax though
a very cool instrument.
Ever hear Clarence in the E Street Band?

Coat of Arms

In Boston's Back Bay up the street from
the famous Cheers Bar I almost step
on a manhole cover with one word
inscribed across its center: *Estabrook*

What the hell? What could that be?
a company name?
an early family marker?
the cover over the underground East Brook?

Take a picture with my fancy iPhone email it
to my brothers and an assortment of other Estabrooks
across the country:
Anybody have any ideas
what it means, where it might have come from?

Within minutes I have my answer, mystery solved
by my Cousin Billy in upstate New York:
"that cousin is our family's coat of arms
now let's get together some night
and put the grab on this baby
tell me that wouldn't look grand
hangin' on the family room wall"

Pepsi and a Package of Planters Salted Peanuts

Five-hours dodging trucks and traffic
stupid drivers and old people
putt-putting along
in the rain. You arrive finally
check in to Holiday Inn Express
off exit 9 of Turnpike

Hang up your clothes
keep them wrinkle-free
old "on the road" salesman habit

Then you buy a Pepsi
from the vending machine (you prefer Coke
but sometimes there isn't a choice)
and a one-ounce package
of Planters Salted Peanuts

Pull off your shoes
plop your feet up on the desk
eat and drink
the room quiet and dim like a mausoleum
when have you ever felt better?

Do not go gentle into that good night.

Dylan Thomas (1914-1953)

Shirtless at Mid-day
95 degrees time to climb the ladder finish painting
the gutter and overhang. I enjoy taunting the gods
they've been at me 70 years already!

Old Weightlifter
Lifting heavy barbells at 70
knowing he can seriously injure himself
a risk he's willing to take
to feel young
and strong again.

Rigged
He hates growing old, aching joints, slipping eyesight
and memory, but fights it constantly even knowing
the game is rigged and the gods
will have their way.

Fate

I step over a penny in the street
Dad you can't leave it there bring it home save it
it's bad luck if you don't

Okay honey I didn't know
I pick it up promptly, drop it through a sewer grate

Dad No! She stops and stares her hand over her mouth

Bring it on you bastards! Come and get me!
I yell to whoever these vindictive petty
penny-pinching gods might be

www.ingramcontent.com/pod-product-compliance
Lightning Source LLC
LaVergne TN
LVHW051500170726
843492LV00002B/740